SOCIAL & EMOTIONAL LEARNING CURRICULUM

By Mary Birdsell and Jo Meserve Mach

FINDING MY WORLD
The Finding My World book series presents nonfiction, multi-cultural, and geographically diverse books that give voice to children with disabilities. Inclusive stories offer students the opportunity to meet children and adults with disabilities.

SEL CURRICULUM
The Finding My World literature-based SEL curriculum promotes the development of skills needed for social awareness. Lessons combine social, emotional learning with story time and activities based on components defined in the CASEL social-awareness competency.

© 2021 Mary Birdsell, Jo Meserve Mach

These activities may be reproduced solely for classroom use and may not be used or posted online.

Finding My World SEL Curriculum

Finding My Way Books
3512 SW Huntoon St.
Topeka, Kansas 66604
www.findingmywaybooks.com

(785) 273-6239

ISBN: 978-1-94754-137-5

Printed in the United States

10 9 8 7 6 5 4 3 2 1

For more information or to contact the author, please go to www.findingmywaybooks.com.

SEL CURRICULUM   FINDING MY WORLD BOOK SERIES

> The **Finding My World** book series presents nonfiction, multi-cultural, and geographically diverse books that give voice to children with disabilities. Inclusive stories offer students the opportunity to meet children and adults with disabilities.

We have linked a book to the self-awareness competency for each SEL lesson. Students will gain context for each competency by reading the stories, learning story background information, learning about different disability diagnoses, answering three styles of discussion questions, and completing activities.

Social and Emotional Learning

Social awareness: The abilities to understand the perspectives of and empathize with others, including those from diverse backgrounds, cultures, & contexts. This includes the capacities to feel compassion for others, understand broader historical and social norms for behavior in different settings, and recognize family, school, and community resources and supports. Such as:

- *Taking others' perspectives*
- *Recognizing strengths in others*
- *Demonstrating empathy and compassion*
- *Showing concern for the feelings of others*
- *Understanding and expressing gratitude*
- *Identifying diverse social norms, including unjust ones*
- *Recognizing situational demands and opportunities*
- *Understanding the influence of organizations/systems on behaviors*

CASEL 2020

ABOUT THE CO-AUTHORS AND PHOTOGRAPHER

Mary Birdsell has authored nine children's books and is a former Speech and Theatre teacher with an enthusiasm for all styles of learners. Mary believes everyone learns, creates, and has a story to tell. As a photographer, she strives to create images that reflect the strengths of each child. She uses colors and shapes to tell a story. For her, each book is like its own theater production.

Jo **Meserve Mach** is co-author of the Finding My Way book set. She is very passionate about sharing the stories of children with special needs after working 36 years as an Occupational Therapist. Jo embraces the joy that individuals with disabilities bring to our communities through their unique gifts.

Finding My World book set: SEL Teacher's Guide

Table of Contents

Claire Wants a Boxing Name 1
    Boxing Moves 2
    The Best Name Ever 3

Neema Wants to Learn 4
    Discovering Opportunities 6
    Teach a Game 7

Onika Wants to Help 8
    Being Included 10
    What in the World 11

Matteo Wants to See What's Next 12
    Organize Matteo's Museum Visit 14
    A Fun Wheelchair Accessible Place 15

Cooper Wants to Do Chores 16
    Taking Care of Animals 18
    Accepting Different Feelings 19

MyaGrace Wants to Get Ready 20
    Helping MyaGrace Get Ready 22
    Thank You 23

Claire's Word Find 24

Neema's Word Find 25

Onika's Word Find 26

Matteo's Word Find 27

Cooper's Word Find 28

MyaGrace's Word Find 29

Finding My World SEL Activities Key 30

SEL Student Survey 34

Data Collection 35

Social Awareness Award 36

SEL CURRICULUM — CLAIRE WANTS A BOXING NAME

Genre: Nonfiction
GRL: M
Interest level: K-4
Lexile: 470L

SEL social awareness competency:
recognizing strengths in others

Disabilities represented:
facial difference, differently sight-abled

Vocabulary:
boxing
attention
harness
owner
focus
cartwheel

The **Finding My World** book series presents nonfiction, multi-cultural, and geographically diverse books that give voice to children with disabilities. Inclusive stories offer students the opportunity to meet children and adults with disabilities.

Summary

Claire lives in Toronto and knows that women at the Toronto Newsgirls Boxing Club have really cool boxing names. They have names like Slice 'n Dice and Eraser. Getting a boxing name is a great honor. After she shows her coach Vivian how well she is learning to box, Claire hopes she gets her name today.

Background

We photographed Claire's story when she was 10 years old. She speaks both English and French. She loves singing, dancing, swimming, skating, and tumbling. Claire was born with a facial difference. Occasionally, she has to explain her appearance to others, but she doesn't let this limit her.

> A **craniofacial difference** refers to an abnormality of the face and/or the head. Craniofacial differences can result from abnormal growth patterns of the face or skull, which involves soft tissue and bones. cdc.gov

Vivian immigrated from Hong Kong to Canada. She had an injury which caused her loss of sight. Vivian describes herself as "differently sight-abled." She has a service dog named Catcher.

Vivian helped write Claire's story by contributing her perspective as a coach and mentor. She wanted Claire to learn the value of paying attention because she believes that paying attention strengthens abilities.

Vivian spends a lot of time paying attention to what she is doing. It took her two years to understand her body sensations when she was boxing. She learned the placement of her hands and the timing of when to punch the bag. When shadow boxing, she pays attention to the distance between her feet and the sound of her movements.

> "I believe Claire is already physically strong, but what makes a good human being is being physically, emotionally, and mentally strong. When she has finished eight weeks of coaching, she'll be a focused individual, and then she will earn her boxing name!" Vivian, Claire's boxing coach

Social awareness competency: recognizing strengths in others

SEL CURRICULUM   CLAIRE WANTS A BOXING NAME

Pre-Reading Questions

1. Hold up the front cover. Why is this book nonfiction?
2. What do you think the story could be about?
3. What is Claire doing on the cover?
4. Hold up the back cover. What do you think the shapes mean?
5. Read the back of the book. Where is Toronto? How far away is it?
6. What is a facial difference?
7. What does it mean to be differently sight-abled?
8. What does a boxing gym look like?

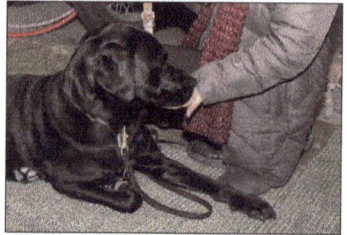

Discussion Questions

1. What are the benefits of boxing?
2. How do you think Vivian learned how to box?
3. What would being differently sight abled be like?
4. What kinds of things would you do at a boxing gym?
5. Would you want Vivian to teach you to box?
6. Why does Claire look up to Vivian?
7. Who do you look up to?
8. Is there a difference between women and men boxing?

Comprehension Questions

1. What does Claire like about boxing?
2. How does Catcher know when he has to work?
3. Why would someone want a boxing name?
4. What do Claire, her mom, and Vivian do to warm-up?
5. How does Claire learn from Vivian?
6. What is shadow boxing?
7. Why do boxers wrap their hands?
8. What are some different kinds of boxing bags?

Activities

Boxing Moves
This activity gives students the opportunity to make cubes to use in playing a game with their peers. Label the cube with different boxing moves and thrown like a die.

The Best Name Ever
This activity gives students the opportunity to recognize their friends' strengths. Students think of boxing names for three friends and explain why they chose each name.

Claire's Word Find offers some extra fun on page 24.

Social awareness competency: recognizing strengths in others

Claire Wants a Boxing Name

Boxing Moves

Name_____ Date_____

Cut out the pattern below to make a cube. On each of the six squares, write one of the following words: cartwheel, blender, push-up, shadow box, 1-2-3-4-5-6 POW, and take a break. Take turns rolling your cube. Do the activity that is on top or ask someone who you know is good at that activity to do it.

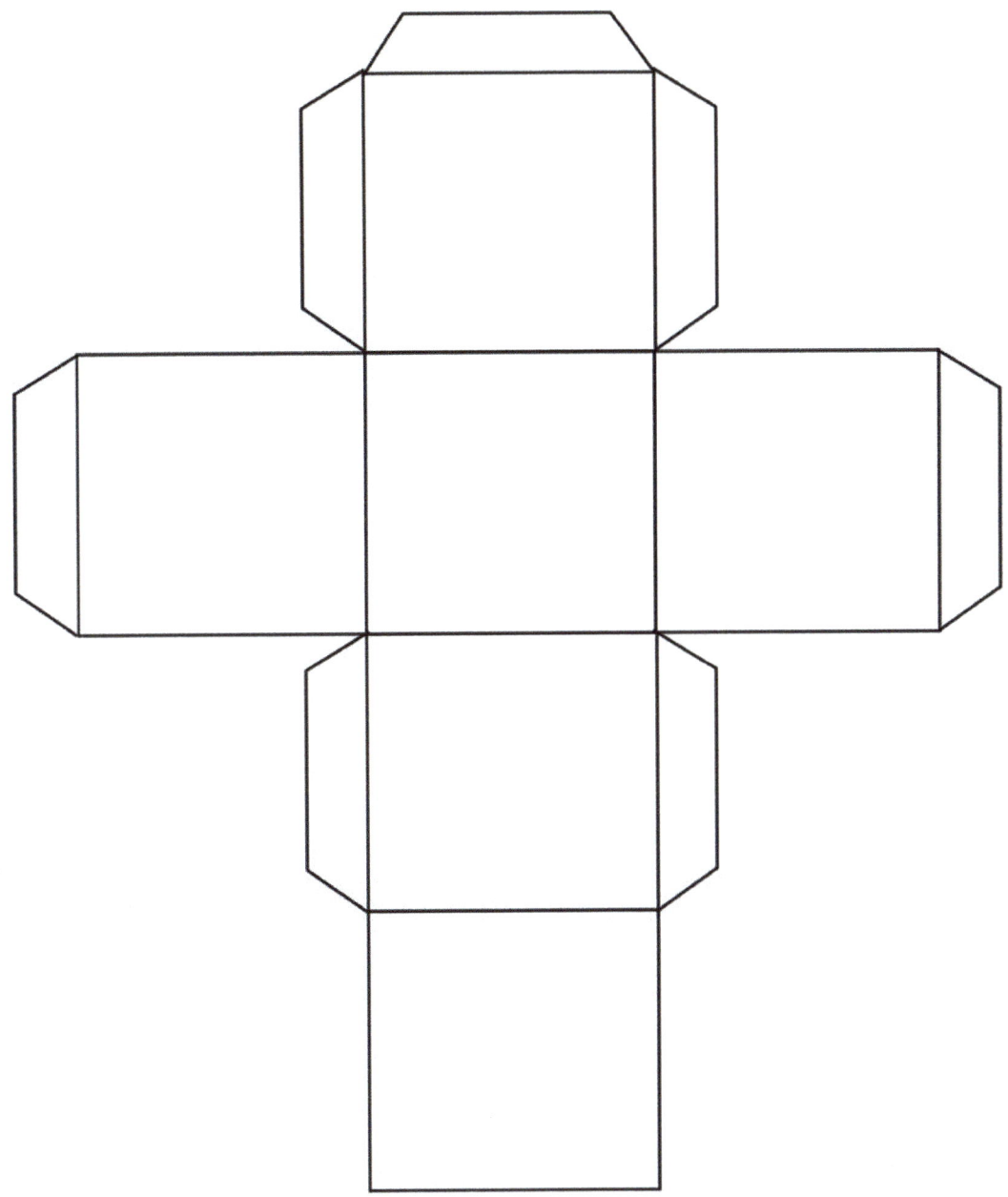

Social awareness competency: recognizing strength in others

Claire Wants a Boxing Name

The Best Name Ever

Name_____   Date_____

Claire's coach, Vivian, spent a lot of time choosing a boxing name for Claire. She wanted a name to show Claire's ability to focus. Some names she considered were Cannonball, Dynamite, Shooting Star, Grasshopper, Spark Plug, and Firecracker. Claire worried they would give her the name Claire Cartwheel, but she got the best name ever!

Give amazing names to three of your friends, based on their strengths. Think about what each friend is good at doing. Fill in the sentence to explain how you chose their name.

Friend   **Best Name Ever!**

I chose _____ because _____

_____.

I chose _____ because _____

_____.

I chose _____ because _____

_____.

Social awareness competency: recognizing strengths in others

SEL CURRICULUM NEEMA WANTS TO LEARN

Genre: Nonfiction
GRL: M
Interest level: K-4
Lexile: 470L

SEL social awareness competency:
recognizing situational demands and opportunities

Disability represented:
learning disability

Vocabulary:
coconut
encourage
trick
attention
orphanage
grate

The **Finding My World** book series presents nonfiction, multi-cultural, and geographically diverse books that give voice to children with disabilities. Inclusive stories offer students the opportunity to meet children and adults with disabilities.

Summary
Neema lives in Tanzania and is having a busy day. She plays ball with Mama Mdemu and Joseph. She helps fix lunch. She completes her homework. She helps take care of the smaller children and she teaches Joseph a new game. Neema is learning all day long and discovers what she would like to do when she grows up.

Background
We photographed Neema's book when she was 11 years old and her friend Joseph was 12 years old. Neema has a learning disability.

Neema is an orphan living at the Irente Children's Home in Lushoto, Tanzania. Mama Mdemu is the director of this home. She began her position after retiring from a career in nursing.

Neema is social and likes to welcome visitors to the orphanage. She speaks English and Swahili. Neema also likes to help take care of younger

> *Learning disabilities* are differences in a person's brain that can affect how well they read, write, speak, do math, and handle other similar tasks. Having a learning disability, or even several disabilities, isn't related to intelligence. It just means that the person's brain works differently from others. nichd.nih.gov

children in the orphanage. She helps feed them, and she also does laundry.

When Neema goes to school, she wears a uniform. It's Saturday in her book, so she is wearing clothes she chose that day. Young women can go to the school Neema attends and learn to become childcare workers. This school is important in Tanzania because it gives young women an education and training for a job.

Both Neema and Joseph have learned to read and write in Swahili and English.

Social awareness competency: recognizing situational demands and opportunities

SEL CURRICULUM   NEEMA WANTS TO LEARN

Pre-Reading Questions

1. Hold up the front cover. Why is this book nonfiction?
2. What do you think the story could be about?
3. What is Neema doing on the cover?
4. Hold up the back cover. What do you think the colors mean?
5. Read the back of the book. Where is Tanzania? How far away is it?
6. What is a learning disability?
7. What is the geography of Tanzania?

Discussion Questions

1. What does Neema like about Saturdays?
2. What do you have in common with Neema?
3. How would your day be different if you lived in an orphanage?
4. When you play with younger children, how do you help them?
5. What is your favorite subject? What subject is more challenging?
6. Why would Neema make a good teacher?
7. What kind of opportunities does Neema have?
8. How are they the same as yours? How are they different?

Comprehension Questions

1. What kind of home does Neema live in?
2. Why do you think so many children live there?
3. What day of the week is it?
4. What types of games do Neema and Mama Mdemu play?
5. What does Joseph like to play?
6. What is Neema's favorite food?
7. How does she help cook?
8. What is Neema's favorite subject?

Activities

Discovering Opportunities

This activity promotes awareness of how students can discover opportunities for personal growth in everyday activities.

Teach a Game

This activity shows students how to teach a game to someone who has a learning disability. It encourages students to think about how to best support others.

Neema's Word Find offers some extra fun on page 25.

Social awareness competency: recognizing situational demands and opportunities

Neema Wants to Learn

Discovering Opportunities

Name_____   Date_____

Neema is very busy. She plays ball and jumps rope. She helps fix lunch. She does her schoolwork. She helps take care of the younger children. Neema looks at each of these tasks as opportunities to learn. Mama Mdemu is often her teacher. Sometimes, Joseph is her teacher.

Here is an example of one of Neema's opportunities.

Doing an activity
Mama Mdemu taught Neema how to play a game. Neema plays it with Mama Mdemu and Joseph.

↓

Thinking about the activity
Neema thought about how she learned to play a game. She decided she wanted to teach someone how to play a game.

↓

Taking an opportunity
Neema makes up her own game and teaches it to Joseph.

Write about when you found an opportunity.

Doing an activity

↓

Thinking about the activity

↓

Taking an opportunity

Social awareness competency: recognizing situational demands and opportunities

Neema Wants to Learn

Teach a Game

Name_____   Date_____

Neema taught Joseph a game she plays by herself. Think of a game that you play by yourself. Draw pictures of your game so it is easier for someone who has a hard time reading to understand. Add one or two words to explain your pictures.

1_____   2_____

3_____   4_____

Social awareness competency: recognizing situational demands and opportunities

SEL CURRICULUM   ONIKA WANTS TO HELP

Genre: Nonfiction
GRL: M
Interest level: K-4
Lexile: 480L

SEL Social awareness competency: identifying diverse social norms, including unjust one

Disabilities represented: intellectual disabilities, autism spectrum disorder or ASD

Vocabulary:
rain forest
prepare
market
swish
talent
village

The **Finding My World** book series presents nonfiction, multi-cultural, and geographically diverse books that give voice to children with disabilities. Inclusive stories offer students the opportunity to meet children and adults with disabilities.

Summary
Onika and her friends are learning jobs at their school in Tanzania. They each discover their talent and that helps them choose where they want to work. Onika shows all she has learned. However, it's not until the end of her story that she shares her talent.

Background
When Onika was a little girl, her community wanted children with disabilities hidden so no one would see them. In 2003, the parents of all the children with disabilities got together and said they wanted their children to go to school. The church council helped them build a school. They asked people all around the country for help.

Intellectual disability is a term used when there are limits to a person's ability to learn at an expected level and function in daily life. Levels of intellectual disability vary greatly in children. cdc.gov

People gave money, building supplies, and volunteered to help build the school. Some grew potatoes and peppers that they sold to help raise money.

In 2005, the Rainbow School opened. They named it for rainbows because rainbows represent safety and hope to families. In 2009, the school added classes to help students learn to do a job. Onika's book shows the new classes.

People with ASD often have problems with social, emotional, and communication skills. They might repeat certain behaviors and might not want change in their daily activities. Many people with ASD also have different ways of learning, paying attention, or reacting to things. cdc.gov

In 2014, the school got safe drinking water. By 2015, they had 35 students at Rainbow School.

Social awareness competency: identifying diverse social norms, including unjust ones

SEL CURRICULUM ONIKA WANTS TO HELP

Pre-Reading Questions

1. Hold up the front cover. Why is this book nonfiction?
2. What do you think the story could be about?
3. What is Onika doing on the cover?
4. Hold up the back cover. What do you think the colors mean?
5. Read the back of the book. Where is Tanzania? How far away is it?
6. What is an intellectual disability?
7. What is autism or ASD?
8. What is the geography of Tanzania?

Discussion Questions

1. Why didn't Onika get to go to school when she was little?
2. Is it right that Onika didn't get to go to school when she was young?
3. How is Onika's school different from your school?
4. How is Onika's school similar to yours?
5. What do you think Onika, Teo, Elibeth, and Agnes like about their school?
6. How can you tell they like the school?
7. What does your school do to help your community?
8. What could you learn at school that would help your community?

Comprehension Questions

1. Where does Onika live?
2. Did Onika get to go to school when she was little?
3. What kind of things do Onika and her friends do at school?
4. What does Teo love to do?
5. What do Elibeth and Agnes love to do?
6. What is their kitchen like?
7. How does Onika help in the kitchen?
8. What is Onika's favorite thing to do?

Activities

Being Included
This activity encourages students to explore feelings of exclusion and inclusion.

What in the World?
This activity enhances student awareness of unjust social norms and empowers students to consider their ability to influence social norms.

Onika's Word Find offers extra fun on page 26.

Social awareness competency: identifying diverse social norms, including unjust ones

Onika Wants to Help

Being Included

Name_____   Date_____

Often, social norms are about excluding people. In Onika's story, she and her friends were excluded from going to school because they had disabilities. A norm might be that the oldest person always gets to go first, or the fastest person gets to do errand, or that only boys get to play a certain game.

Think about inclusion. Maybe all ages of people want to take turns going first. Maybe, slower runners can do errands and learn to run faster. Maybe girls could play that game, too.

When have you been excluded? _____

How did you feel? _____

Do you think you should have been included? Why? _____

_____

Draw a picture of how you feel when you are **excluded**.	Draw a picture of how you feel when you are **included**.

Social awareness competency: identifying diverse social norms, including unjust ones

Onika Wants to Help

What in the World?

Name_____   Date_____

Sometimes, people think they should do something because everyone living within their culture does it. For example, in Onika's culture, only children without disabilities went to school. Sometimes, when you learn about social norms, you want to say, "*What in the world were they thinking?*"

Here's a crazy world full of crazy norms.

You must have black curly hair to go to school.

You must have a million dollars to swim in the ocean.

You must be taller than five feet to get a pet.

You must be able to speak Spanish to drive a car.

List two norms to make a better world.

1._____

_____

2. _____

_____

Social awareness competency: identifying diverse social norms, including unjust ones

SEL CURRICULUM — MATTEO WANTS TO SEE WHAT'S NEXT

Genre: Nonfiction
GRL: M
Interest level: K-4
Lexile: 490L

SEL social awareness competency:
understanding the influences of organizations/systems on behavior

Disability represented: cerebral palsy

Vocabulary:
museum
docent
eye gaze
opossum
pterodactyls
Buddha

The **Finding My World** book series presents nonfiction, multi-cultural, and geographically diverse books that give voice to children with disabilities. Inclusive stories offer students the opportunity to meet children and adults with disabilities.

Summary

Matteo and Cristian are brothers living in Toronto. They enjoy spending time with their friend Rebecca. Today, they choose to visit the Royal Ontario museum together. Rebecca is a docent at the museum. She has cerebral palsy and uses nonverbal communication to help them explore museum exhibits and discover an exciting new display.

Background

We photographed their story when Matteo was in 1st grade, and Cristian was in 3rd grade. They are both bilingual. They speak English and French.

Rebecca has cerebral palsy and is nonverbal. She uses a power chair for movement. Rebecca communicates with her eye gaze and facial expressions.

Rebecca grew up attending regular classrooms. Her peers helped her take part in their activities. For example, when a group jumped rope, one girl realized that if they flipped the jump rope back and forth over Rebecca's head, she could jump rope with them.

She and Anna, the mother of Matteo and Cristian, are best friends. They both dance professionally. Rebecca dances with the *Spirit Movers*, a group that includes people with disabilities and the people who assist them. Anna and Rebecca danced for Pope John Paul II during the celebration of World Youth Day.

Cerebral palsy (CP) *is a group of disorders that affect a person's ability to move and maintain balance and posture. CP is the most common motor disability in childhood.* Cerebral *means having to do with the brain.* Palsy *means weakness or problems with using the muscles.* cdc.gov

In 2005 at the United Nations, Rebecca gave a PowerPoint presentation on the importance of inclusion. The committee she presented to was drafting their declaration on the rights of people with disabilities.

Social awareness competency: understanding the influences of organizations/systems on behavior

SEL CURRICULUM — MATTEO WANTS TO SEE WHAT'S NEXT

Pre-Reading Questions

1. Hold up the front cover. Why is this book nonfiction?
2. What do you think the story could be about?
3. What is Matteo looking at on the cover?
4. Hold up the back cover. What do you think the colors mean?
5. Read the back of the book. Where is the Royal Ontario Museum? How far away is it?
6. What is cerebral palsy?
7. What does a crystal look like? Could a building look like a crystal? Look at page 11.

Discussion Questions

1. Why do Matteo and Cristian like going to the museum with Rebecca?
2. Have you ever been to a museum?
3. Is the Royal Ontario Museum similar to a museum near you?
4. How do you behave at a museum? Why is that appropriate?
5. What kinds of exhibits would you want to see?
6. How could those exhibits be interactive?
7. What could a museum do to make exhibits/activities for people who have different needs? (multiple languages on pg. 13, ramps on pg. 15, objects on walls and ceilings on pg. 26)

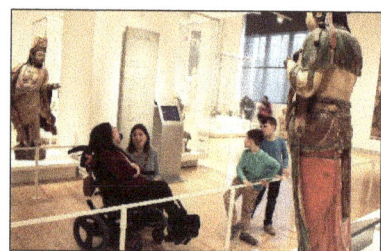

Comprehension Questions

1. How do Matteo and Cristian decide what to do?
2. Why does Rebecca have a different way of communicating?
3. What is Rebecca's job?
4. What do Matteo and Cristian like about the biodiversity exhibit?
5. What kinds of animals do Matteo and Cristian touch?
6. What part of the museum is new to Matteo and Cristian?
7. What types of things do Matteo and Cristian see in the China exhibit?
8. What is Rebecca's surprise for Matteo and Cristian?

Activities

Organize Matteo's Museum Visit
This activity asks students to sequence the exhibits Matteo visited and to think of a new exhibit.

A Fun Wheelchair Accessible Place
This activity expands students' understanding of accessibility and encourages their awareness of how they can help alter an environment to make it more accessible.

Matteo's Word Find offers some extra fun on page 27.

Social awareness competency: understanding the influences of organizations/systems on behavior

Matteo Wants to See What's Next

Organize Matteo's Museum Visit

Name_____   Date_____

Matteo and Cristian visited many exhibits during their trip to the Royal Ontario Museum. Matteo kept wanting to see what was next, because he wanted to see his surprise.

Number the exhibits below in the order Matteo and Cristian visited them.

_____ pterodactyl

_____ snake skin

_____ forest

_____ China

_____ T. rex

_____ bat cave

Draw a symbol for an exhibit you would like to visit at a museum. Label your symbol.

_____

Social awareness competency: understanding the influences of organizations/systems on behavior

Matteo Wants to See What's Next

A Fun Wheelchair Accessible Place

Name_____   Date _____

The Royal Ontario Museum is an accessible museum. Rebecca could move around easily in her wheelchair. Think about what makes a place accessible.

Circle the words that describe a place that would be accessible and fun for someone in a wheelchair.

stairs

smooth paths

ladders

rocky paths

dark so it's difficult to see

tables

things piled on the floor

good light so it's easy to see

nothing on the floor

fun objects hanging at shoulder height

soft and cuddly objects to hold

narrow doorways

crowded with people

objects on high shelves

ramps

What else could be added to a wheelchair accessible place?

_____

_____

Social awareness competency: understanding the influences of organizations/systems on behaviors

SEL CURRICULUM   COOPER WANTS TO DO CHORES

Genre: Nonfiction
GRL: N
Interest level: K-4
Lexile: 520L

SEL Social awareness competency:
demonstrating empathy and compassion

Disabilities represented: arthrogryposis, TAR syndrome

Vocabulary:
chore
pitch
plunger
accidentally
hay bale
pitchfork

The **Finding My World** book series presents nonfiction, multi-cultural, and geographically diverse books that give voice to children with disabilities. Inclusive stories offer students the opportunity to meet children and adults with disabilities.

Summary

Cooper lives on a farm in rural America. His family keeps busy doing chores and Cooper wants to help. They have many chores to care for their sheep to keep them healthy. Cooper, his older brother, and his parents all work together to get their chores done.

Background

We photographed Cooper's story when he was seven years old and beginning 2nd grade.

Cooper was born with arthrogryposis and TAR syndrome. Throughout his life, he's had many surgeries and a lot of therapy to help him move his joints so he can walk and use his arms.

Arthrogryposis refers to the development of multiple joint contractures affecting two or more areas of the body prior to birth. A contracture occurs when a joint becomes permanently fixed in a bent or straightened position, which can impact the function and range of motion of the joint. nih.gov

The year before his book, he had leg surgery and spent seven months in a wheelchair before he could walk again. We planned the writing and photographing of his story around his surgeries, so he could show all that he can do with his family as they take care of their sheep.

Cooper may have physical limitations, but that doesn't stop him from being bright and active. His nickname is Super Cooper.

Cooper likes to play tug of war with their dog Lucie. He also likes to swing high and run fast.

TAR syndrome is characterized by the absence of a bone called the radius in each forearm and short stature. nih.gov

Social awareness competency: demonstrating empathy and compassion

SEL CURRICULUM — COOPER WANTS TO DO CHORES

Pre-Reading Questions

1. Hold up the front cover. Why is this book nonfiction?
2. What do you think the story could be about?
3. What is Cooper doing on the cover?
4. Hold up the back cover. What do you think the colors mean?
5. Read the back of the book. What is a farm?
6. What is arthrogryposis?
7. What is TAR syndrome?
8. What does a farm look like?

Discussion Questions

1. Why does it take a whole family to do chores on a farm?
2. Why does Cooper like living on a farm?
3. Would you want to live on a farm? Why or why not?
4. What do the lambs do when they feel anxious?
5. How do you know when you feel anxious? What do you do?
6. Why does Cooper tell the lamb that they are sorry? Would you be sorry too?
7. How can you tell Cooper cares about the animals?
8. How can you show animals and people that you care about them?

Comprehension Questions

1. Where does Cooper live?
2. What kinds of chores are there on a farm?
3. How does Cooper tell the difference between girl and boy lambs?
4. What do lambs do when they feel anxious?
5. Why is it important for the lambs to get their medicine?
6. What happens if lambs' hooves get too long?
7. What do lambs eat?
8. What is Cooper's favorite chore? Why?

Activities

Taking Care of Animals
This activity encourages students to recall Cooper's chores and their chores caring for a pet.

Accepting Different Feelings
This activity facilitates student awareness of their automatic feelings about different animals.

Cooper's Word Find offers some extra fun on page 28.

Social awareness competency: demonstrating empathy and compassion

Cooper Wants to Do Chores

Taking Care of Animals

Name_____   Date_____

Cooper and his family work hard taking care of their sheep. Do you remember their chores?

1. Circle the chores they do.
2. Put a check mark in front of the chores you would do if you were taking care of a pet.

_____   brush their hair

_____   feed them

_____   give them medicine

_____   trim their hooves or nails

_____   tag them so you can keep track of them

_____   pet them

_____   take them for walks

_____   give them baths

Social awareness competency: demonstrating empathy and compassion

19

Cooper Wants to Do Chores

Accepting Different Feelings

Name_____   Date_____

What do you feel when you see a dog?

Maybe you get excited because you love dogs and have a dog you play with at home.

Maybe you get scared because a dog bit you.

Maybe you get happy because dogs love to lick you and give you doggy kisses.

Based on our experiences, we all have different feelings. It's important to accept how others feel and be kind to them. We don't know why they feel a certain way, but we can still accept those feelings.

For this activity, write your feelings about something and then ask someone else their feelings about the same thing. Compare your feelings and know that both of your feelings are okay.

1. What do you feel when you see a cat? Why?

What does someone else feel when they see a cat? Why?

Are your feelings the same? _____   Are your feelings different? _____

2. What do you feel when it's raining? Why?

What does some else feel when it's raining? Why?

Are your feelings the same? _____   Are your feelings different? _____

Social awareness competency: demonstrating empathy and compassion

SEL CURRICULUM — MYAGRACE WANTS TO GET READY

The **Finding My World** book series presents nonfiction, multi-cultural, and geographically diverse books that give voice to children with disabilities. Inclusive stories offer students the opportunity to meet children and adults with disabilities.

Genre: Nonfiction
GRL: N
Interest level: K-4
Lexile: 530L

SEL social awareness competency:
understanding and expressing gratitude

Disabilities represented:
cerebral palsy, intellectual disability

Vocabulary:
message
get ready
practice
list
surprise
makeup

Summary

MyaGrace lives in suburban America. Her school is having a big dance, and she wants to go with her friend Emily. Getting permission and then getting ready keeps her very busy. She has so many decisions to make! She needs to choose a dress, shoes, and jewelry. Plus, she needs time to practice dancing with her brother. Mom makes plans, too, for a trip to the beauty salon for MyaGrace.

Background

An American family adopted MyaGrace from India when she was two years old. She was tiny for her age and had difficulty eating. Today, she is an enthusiastic teenager, wanting to experience life as fully as possible.

MyaGrace has cerebral palsy and intellectual disabilities. Her family helps support her in the activities she chooses. MyaGrace especially loves activities that include dancing and music.

Cerebral palsy (CP) is a group of disorders that affect a person's ability to move and maintain balance and posture. CP is the most common motor disability in childhood. Cerebral means having to do with the brain. Palsy means weakness or problems with using the muscles. cdc.gov

When MyaGrace asked her mom if she could attend the school dance, her mom could have said yes and made all the plans for her. Instead, her mom encouraged her participation. As a result, MyaGrace learned many new skills.

Intellectual disability is a term used when there are limits to a person's ability to learn at an expected level and function in daily life. Levels of intellectual disability vary greatly in children. cdc.gov

MyaGrace wants you to know that she danced to every song and had a wonderful time at her school dance.

Social awareness competency: understanding and expressing gratitude

SEL CURRICULUM — MYAGRACE WANTS TO GET READY

Pre-Reading Questions

1. Hold up the front cover. Why is this book nonfiction?
2. What do you think the story could be about?
3. What is MyaGrace doing on the cover?
4. Hold up the back cover. What do you think the colors mean?
5. Read the back of the book. Have you been to a school dance?
6. What is cerebral palsy?
7. What are intellectual disabilities?
8. What is it like to go to a dance?

Discussion Questions

1. Why does MyaGrace want to go to the dance?
2. Would you want to go to a dance? Why or why not?
3. How would you get ready for a dance?
4. Who would you ask to help you get ready for the dance? Why?
5. What does it feel like to be grateful?
6. How do you thank people who have helped you?
7. Why is it important to thank people?
8. How does it feel when someone thanks you?

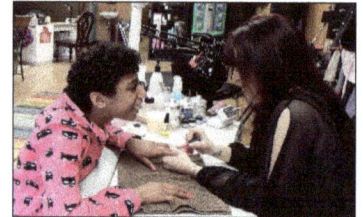

Comprehension Questions

1. What does MyaGrace like to do with music?
2. Who invites MyaGrace to the school dance?
3. What does MyaGrace need to do to get ready for the dance?
4. How does MyaGrace pick a dress to wear?
5. Who helps MyaGrace with her nails and hair?
6. What does MyaGrace's mom surprise her with?
7. Why does MyaGrace use a list to get ready for the dance?
8. Who does MyaGrace thank for helping her get ready for the dance?

Activities

Helping MyaGrace Get Ready
This activity encourages students to recall who helped MyaGrace.

Thank You
This activity encourages students to identify people in their lives who help them. Students learn how to write a thank you note.

MyaGrace's Word Find offers some extra fun on page 29.

Social awareness competency: understanding and expressing gratitude

MyaGrace Wants to Get Ready

Helping MyaGrace Get Ready

Name_____   Date_____

MyaGrace had four people help her get ready for her school dance. Can you remember who they were?

Think about how she could thank each of them for helping her. There are many ways you can show someone you appreciate their help. You can help them, give them a surprise or treat, or tell them how you feel.

Who called MyaGrace? _____

How did she help MyaGrace? _____

How did she help MyaGrace at the end of the story? _____
_____

Who helped MyaGrace find her dress? _____

What else did she help MyaGrace find? _____

Who danced with MyaGrace? _____

How did that help her get ready? _____
_____

Who fixed MyaGrace's hair? _____

How else did she help MyaGrace? _____
_____

How could MyaGrace thank each of these people? _____
_____
_____
_____

Social awareness competency: understanding and expressing gratitude

MyaGrace Wants to Get Ready

Thank You

Name_____   Date_____

MyaGrace thanked Lori for helping her get ready for the school dance by fixing her hair, nails, and makeup. This made MyaGrace very happy!

Who has been helpful to you? Make a list of four people who have been helpful or very nice to you. On your list, write their name and why you are thankful for them.

Choose one person and write them a thank you note. Don't forget to give it to them!

My List

1. _____

   _____

2. _____

   _____

3. _____

   _____

4. _____

   _____

Thank you note example

                        Date

Dear Mrs. Lopez,

   Thank you for helping me with my homework.

   You are very nice.

   Sincerely,

   Your name

You can draw a picture on your note to make it special.

Social awareness competency: understanding and expressing gratitude

Claire Wants a Boxing Name

Claire's Word Find

Name _____   Date_____

```
B  R  I  N  G  B  O  X  I  N  G  X
P  M  M  B  L  E  N  D  E  R  I  P
Q  V  I  V  I  A  N  M  D  Y  L  U
J  C  A  R  T  W  H  E  E  L  V  N
H  Y  B  B  Y  G  L  O  V  E  S  C
N  M  A  S  G  O  R  O  P  E  D  H
F  H  G  C  L  A  I  R  E  D  M  N
N  C  A  T  C  H  E  R  P  O  W  L
```

Circle the following words in the puzzle. Words are hidden → ↑

BAG	GLOVES
BLENDER	POW
BOXING	PUNCH
CARTWHEEL	RING
CATCHER	ROPE
CLAIRE	VIVIAN

Social awareness competency: recognizing strength in others

25

Neema Wants to Learn

Neema's Word Find

Name_____   Date_____

```
S  N  J  L  P  X  C  L  A  P  B  X
I  E  U  B  O  W  P  R  I  P  A  P
N  E  M  B  R  Y  D  Y  E  W  L  L
G  M  P  C  O  C  O  N  U  T  L  A
L  A  K  T  P  A  S  R  Q  R  A  Y
B  Q  F  Y  E  Q  T  H  R  O  W  P
U  W  B  J  J  O  S  E  P  H  U  Y
L  J  U  R  E  A  D  A  L  T  E  J
```

Circle the following words in the puzzle. Words are hidden → ↑

BALL	PLAY
CLAP	READ
COCONUT	ROPE
JOSEPH	SING
JUMP	THROW
NEEMA	

Social awareness competency: recognizing situational demands and opportunities

Onika Wants to Help

Onika's Word Find

Name_____   Date_____

```
E  V  H  N  R  E  R  I  C  E  A  O
L  G  O  X  J  O  S  E  P  H  G  N
I  E  E  K  Y  A  G  N  E  S  S  I
B  R  F  V  I  L  L  A  G  E  E  K
E  X  S  P  G  A  R  D  E  N  E  A
T  C  A  R  R  O  T  S  I  N  D  R
H  B  E  A  D  S  B  W  G  V  S  V
F  B  K  S  W  I  S  H  M  R  Q  Q
```

Circle the following words in the puzzle. Words are hidden ⟶ ↑

AGNES   ONIKA

BEADS   RICE

CARROTS   SEEDS

ELIBETH   SWISH

GARDEN   VILLAGE

HOE

Social awareness competency: identifying diverse social norms, including unjust ones

Matteo Wants to See What's Next

Matteo's Word Find

Name_____   Date_____

```
C  S  R  E  Q  F  O  R  E  S  T  G
R  M  E  D  I  N  O  S  A  U  R  W
I  A  B  E  L  L  M  Y  V  R  S  D
S  T  E  Q  N  I  A  A  C  P  N  C
T  T  C  C  H  I  N  A  K  R  A  A
I  E  C  M  U  S  E  U  M  I  K  V
A  O  A  D  O  W  L  T  Y  S  E  E
N  G  B  I  M  Y  R  V  H  E  E  H
```

Circle the following words in the puzzle. Words are hidden ⟶ ↑

BELL	MATTEO
CAVE	MUSEUM
CHINA	OWL
CRISTIAN	REBECCA
DINOSAUR	SNAKE
FOREST	SURPRISE

Social awareness competency: understanding the influences of organizations/systems on behavior

Cooper Wants to Do Chores

Cooper's Word Find

Name_____   Date_____

```
G  D  N  H  M  C  S  H  E  E  P  K
D  K  H  O  E  O  G  R  A  I  N  I
P  Z  A  O  D  O  W  E  J  W  U  T
G  J  Y  V  I  P  W  E  R  A  P  T
B  C  L  E  C  E  X  D  O  G  H  E
T  N  Y  S  I  R  V  T  U  L  A  N
B  A  R  N  N  W  E  S  T  O  N  X
C  H  O  R  E  Z  P  A  I  N  T  E
```

Circle the following words in the puzzle. Words are hidden → ↑

BARN	HOOVES
CHORE	KITTEN
COOPER	MEDICINE
DOG	PAINT
GRAIN	SHEEP
HAY	WESTON

Social awareness competency: demonstrating empathy and compassion

MyaGrace Wants to Get Ready

MyaGrace's Word Find

Name_____   Date_____

```
L  I  S  T  W  T  G  Q  P  H  M  D
N  E  C  K  L  A  C  E  U  M  L  R
P  G  Q  O  B  W  I  H  R  A  L  E
N  A  I  L  S  E  E  O  P  K  O  S
A  D  A  N  C  E  M  U  L  E  R  S
G  S  H  O  E  S  O  B  E  U  I  Y
X  E  T  H  A  N  M  O  Q  P  T  F
H  M  Y  A  G  R  A  C  E  I  A  D
```

Circle the following works in the word puzzle. Words are hidden →↑

DANCE	MOM
DRESS	MYAGRACE
ETHAN	NAILS
LIST	NECKLACE
LORI	PURPLE
MAKEUP	SHOES

Social awareness competency: understanding and expressing gratitude

Finding My World book series: SEL Activities Key

Claire Wants a Boxing Name: Claire's Word Find

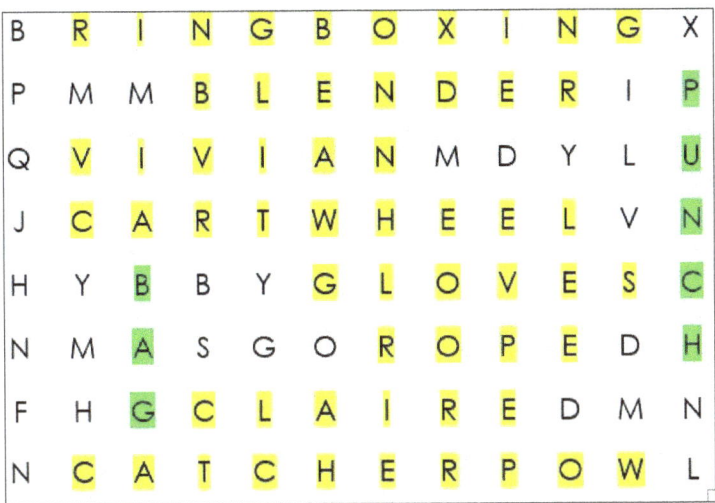

Neema Wants to Learn: Neema's Word Find

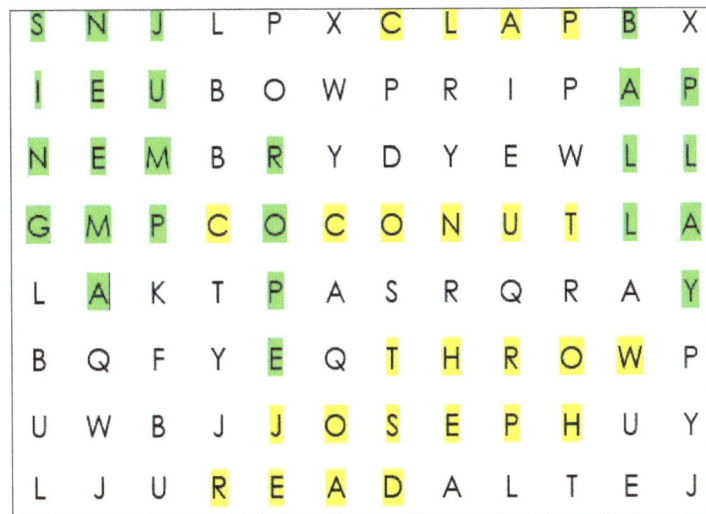

Onika Wants to Help: Onika's Word Find

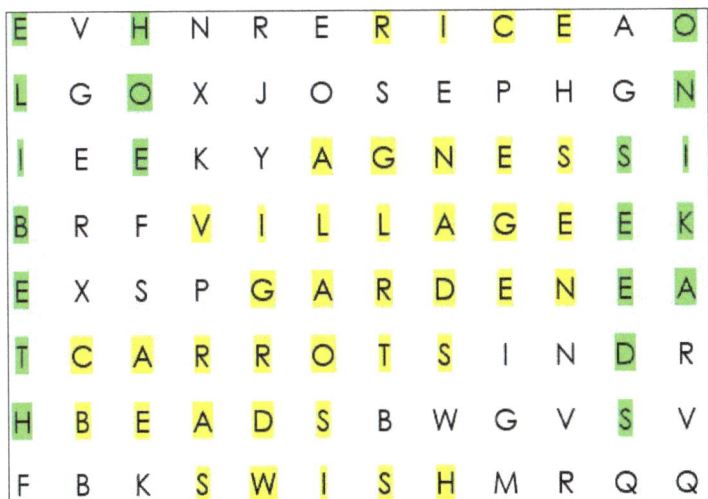

Finding My World book series: SEL Activities Key

Matteo Wants to See What's Next:

Organize Matteo's Museum Visit
1 Forest

2 Snake skin

3 Bat cave

4 China

5 Pterodactyl

6 T-Rex

A Fun Wheelchair Accessible Space
Circle:
stairs

smooth paths

tables

good light

nothing on the floor

fun objects hanging at shoulder height

soft and cuddly objects

ramps

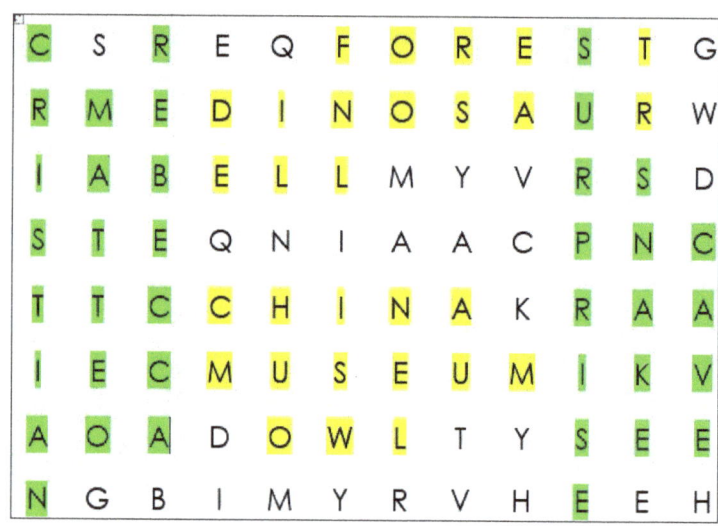

Matteo's Word Find

Cooper Wants to Do Chores:

Taking Care of Animals
  Circle:
   feed them
   give them medicine
   trim their hooves
   tag them

  Check mark:
   brush their hair
   feed them
   pet them
   take them for walks
   give them baths

Cooper's Word Find

Finding My World book series: SEL Activities Key

MyaGrace Wants to Get Ready:

Helping MyaGrace Get Ready

Phone:
  Emily
  ask her to the school dance
  go with her to the school dance

Dress:
  Mom
  shoes
  jewelry

Dance:
  Ethan
  knew she could dance in her dress

Comb:
  Lori
  nails and makeup

MyaGrace's Word Find

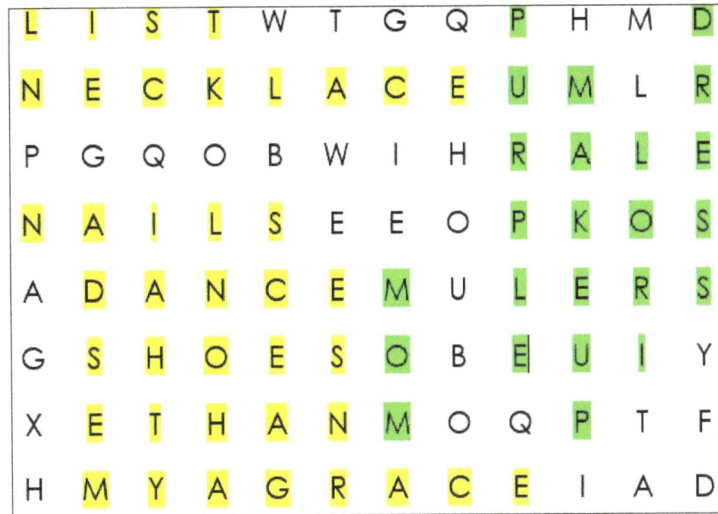

Finding My World SEL Student Survey

Name _____ Date _____ Grade _____

Circle the emoji that best fits you.

	Don't know what to do!	Get nervous. Do nothing.	Smile	Talk
What do I do when I meet someone in a wheelchair?	😳	😐	🙂	😃
What do I do when I meet someone who looks different because of a disability?	😳	😐	🙂	😃
What do I do when I want to play with someone with a disability?	😳	😐	🙂	😃
What do I do when I want to talk to someone I know with a disability?	😳	😐	🙂	😃
How do I feel about being an inclusive friend?	😳	😐	🙂	😃

Data Collection for Finding My World SEL Curriculum

Organization: _____

Number of participants: _____   Pre-survey date: _____   Post-survey date: _____

Description: Each survey contains the following questions with responses selected from an Emoji Likert type scale.

1. What do I do when I meet someone in a wheelchair?
2. What do I do when I meet someone who looks different because of a disability?
3. What do I do when I want to play with someone with a disability?
4. What do I do when I want to talk to someone I know with a disability?
5. How do I feel about being an inclusive friend?

Scoring: Each Emoji has an assigned value. Total the number of responses for each Emoji.
Don't Know what to do! = 1
Get nervous. Do nothing = 2
Smile = 3
Talk = 4

Multiply the number of participants X 5 questions to identify the total number of responses. _____
Divide the number of responses per Emoji by the total to get percentage scores.

Pre-survey:

- _____% of the responses were *'Don't know what to do!'*
- _____% of the responses were *'Get Nervous- Do nothing'*
- _____% of the responses were *'Smile at them'*
- _____% of the responses were *'Talk to them'*

Post-survey:

- _____% of the responses were *'Don't know what to do!'*
- _____% of the responses were *'Get Nervous- Do nothing'*
- _____% of the responses were *'Smile at them'*
- _____% of the responses were *'Talk to them'*

Summary: Compare the pre-and post-survey results to provide a general overview of change in participants attitudes. For additional information you could score each question to identify more specifically where attitude changes occurred. Also, consider including anecdotal data and staff observations during the program.

Finding My World Certificate

Social and Emotional Learning

Social Awareness Award

For understanding how others feel!

Awarded to

_____

_____

Signature and Date